A Handbook for the Performance of English Madrigals

By William Belan with special contributions by Michael Calabrese

Gentry Publications

www.FredBock com

Publishing Editor: Allan Petker
Music Engraver: Dick Bolks

Gentry Publications Catalog No. JG0720
Hal Leonard Catalog no. 08747334
ISBN 8 84088 19245 7

TABLE OF CONTENTS

ACKNOWLEDGMENTS

It would be an exception when only the author is responsible for the book; there is no exception here. In fact, this study is the result of years of influences and scores of individuals who have been both personal inspirations and centers of knowledge. It is these people to whom I am grateful. You may recognize the names of some, while others are unfamiliar. However, all are significant individuals, who have been important to me. In the long-lived tradition of a liturgical litany I put forward their names, and with bright candle light and incense in my imagination, I follow each name with a heartfelt, "I appreciate you:"

Esther Andreas; Hayden Blanchard; Donald Brinegar; Peter F. Drucker; Raymond Egan; Robert M.Fowells; Margaret Hillis; Thomas Lewis; Harold Logan; Otto Werner Mueller; Dennis Shrock; Michael Spiro; Roger Wagner; Donn Weiss; Michael Zearott; my parents and my wife, Gabriela Belan.

Handbook to the English Madrigal

Preface

We intend for this handbook to be useful immediately, for teachers and students, for those who study and perform the madrigal. Further, this handbook is supported by primary and secondary historical sources for the purpose of providing information that assists our readers to sort valid information from personal opinion. Madrigals are a valued body of literature, and when an English madrigal is being prepared for performance one strives to inform the experience with the best information available; thinking through important performance issues of a madrigal builds perspective. Readers of this handbook will receive a unique perspective on the madrigal, the marriage of music and text, and its unique place in the stylistic timeline.

> Therefore, given the alternative between performing as one "feels it," or bringing available knowledge to one's expression, the contemporary performer should feel the obligation of becoming informed.

The assumptions that a conductor makes to form interpretation depend upon the quality of information available. With more than thirty years of combined teaching and research experience, we offer this handbook as a tool for preparing performances of English madrigals. The marriage of music and text that lives in these songs is a very unique relationship, experienced vividly with the guidance of historical materials and responsible scholarship.

English madrigal repertoire remains a popular body of choral literature for choirs because it affords singers, with even modest skills, access to an engaging volume of music. In fact, good amateurs have some advantage over trained professionals with regard to vocal timbre. Amateurs are prone to subordinate sound, to prioritize blend and ensemble, in contrast to the individuality of professional vocal production. It is ideal to have a warm vocal sound, with vibrato that is the result of natural vocal function. Therefore, the madrigal is an ideal repertoire choice for school choirs and community choral societies.

The book is divided into two parts. The first part treats the subject areas of music and poetry. Music considerations deal with the history and meaning of the madrigal, and the stylistic parameters that shape the essence of madrigals. The textual study is an explanation of technical elements of Renaissance poetry as well as suggestions for bringing sensibility to the art of poetics. The second part contains an analysis of two examples of popular English madrigals. Music and poetry from the madrigals are examined and suggestions are made regarding performance decisions. These analyses are given as examples for preparing performances of madrigal music and text, and it is expected that one will infer from these examples how other pieces may be approached and treated. Both sample madrigals are also offered within this text as critical performance editions, in both score and part-book format. These and other select titles are available for purchase through Gentry Publications.

Introduction

Choral performance can be enhanced greatly by the historical study of music. Performance is generally conditioned by our preparation and then becomes an aesthetic image of the research, theory, and practice to be further preserved in rehearsal. In fact, more and more performers of music are becoming proficient in musicological research. The research tools of the past fifty years have created options as to how a piece of music can be approached. Therefore, given the alternative between performing as one "feels" it, or bringing available knowledge to one's expression, the contemporary performer should feel the obligation of becoming informed. For knowledge, when exposed, cannot be denied; not to make use of exposed knowledge deprives oneself and one's audience of a complete performance.

This point of view is not, however, without its detractors who claim that music is only about expressing in the moment and is not to be shaped or otherwise affected by the restrictions of performance practice "rules." Music lives only, so this thinking goes, in the context of modern potential, with its expanded pallet of expression, arsenal of powerful instruments, and broad set of liberties. On the other hand, to the dedicated scholars who have devoted their lives uncovering information, codifying the primary sources, and building a sound ideal that one can replicate, this contemporary point of view appears rather undisciplined.

Music history is a friend to performers. But one's first introduction to history is often a survey of chronological events and thus becomes merely a class to be passed before "real" music making can begin. Perhaps the study of history is first appreciated when one finally awakens to its nested development. When a music student understands that later styles could not exist without previous influences, the world of performance becomes a powerful reality. As conductors, we benefit especially from this paradigm because the entire understanding of musical style depends on "walking forward," not "looking backward." Musicology has devoted itself to this paradigm, recreating for performers a meaningful historical path upon which to progress.

The modern musicologist is a detective, who calls upon both the scientific method and creative intuition. Here is also a philosopher, who understands the nested reality of musical practice, recognizing that from each level of development, which we consider uniquely musical, the next changes even more dramatically. Rather than a simple hierarchy of stylistic principles musical development is actually a *holarchy*: a nested continuum; an actual evolution occurred along this extraordinary continuum.[1]

By the time the English madrigal reached its height of popularity there were already centuries of prior expressive continuum. As far back as Gregorian chant, expression was explicit in its notational system. In the middle of the twentieth century Dom Eugene Cardine, a monk from the Abbye St-Pierre de Solesmes, wrote what has been called the most significant twentieth-century treatise on the performance of chant, on the expression of chant. *Gregorian Semiology*[2] (1970) defines the expressive notation

---

[1] This principle of "integral consciousness" is attributed to Ken Wilber in his series of books including: *One Taste* (2000); *A Brief History of Everything* (1995); *The Marriage of Sense and Soul* (1998).

[2] Dom Eugene Cardine. *Gregorian Semiology,* trans. Robert M. Fowells. Solesmes, France: Abbye St. Pierre de Solesmes, 1982.

of tenth-century unheighened neumes,[3] the manuscript notation that preceded square notation. Further, it codifies in great detail the practice of expression to single notes, or groups of notes, within a given musical phrase, and contributes to unlocking the mystery of chant rhythm. So from the very inception of the musical word expression is seen to be organic. During the next 500 years we witness the continued unfolding of expression, explicit within the practice of music. The evolution of the *tactus* and polyphonic composition, as well as growth in the popularity of secular music, show how each musical stage developed from the level of each preceding influence.

The musicologist is a researcher who makes practical sense of primary sources, those theoretical writings by contemporaries of the time studied, and also of secondary sources, writings that reflect upon primary sources. Armed with this historical knowledge and employing disciplined methodology, the conductor pulls together an understanding of the continuum by following logically a trail of extant materials through knowledge depositories, libraries, museums and private collections, building a tapestry of information into a useful picture.

---

[3] Chironomic-based notation that preserved melody shape, but not specific pitches; largely a reminder to the medieval chant master of a massive repertoire that was otherwise preserved only in oral (aural) traditional.

What is a madrigal?

To the Elizabethans the word *madrigal* was equivalent to a word such as "tissue," a single word that summarizes a form but comes in many different packages, something that you recognize when you see (hear) it. According to Edmond Fellowes, the "madrigal" was a *Ballett, Canzonet, little short Air, Pastoral, Neapolitan, Song* and *Air.* These various "forms" were quite indistinguishable from one another; composers chose to interchange the labels. Byrd used the terms *Pastoral* and *Song;* Orlando Gibbons preferred *motet,* although his pieces were also *madrigals.* Tompkins chose the word *song,* although some of these should have been more accurately entitled *Ballet,* "a vocal composition of the 16th and earth 17th centuries, light in character, but somewhat

> Composers were clearly not focused on formality but rather on the task at hand, to partner with the greatest poets of their time, to set these beautiful words in powerful ways.

in the madrigal style, frequently, in its English form, with a ‘Fa la’ refrain, which could be both sung and danced to; these pieces, says Morley...were ‘commonly called Fa las’."[4] In other words, the term *madrigal* is vague and does not pinpoint a single secular song form. In 1925 Fellowes wrote:

> *In ordinary usage it (madrigal) must be taken to mean that elaborate form of secular song for several voices in combination, which was first introduced by the Flemish composers in Italy towards the middle of the sixteenth century, and was brought to its full development in the same century as the normal type of Italian and English secular part song. It may be further described as a composition for two or more unaccompanied voices singing in combination, all the voice parts being of equal interest and mainly designed from the same melodic material; the words are treated in short phrases which are taken up by the various voices one after another in fugal imitation, and the succeeding phrase is introduced usually after two or three repetitions of the previous phrase, commonly overlapping the one it is displacing, with the result that the introduction of a full close was generally avoided. The subjects dealt with were of every variety, according to the fancy of the composer; many of the madrigals are pastoral in style, but by no means exclusively so; many are set to light lyrics and conventional conceits of an amatory character such as the Elizabethans loved; many also most serious, and a few of these, without being exactly suited to church use, deal with semi-religious subjects. But whatever the subject, the English madrigalist possessed a wonderful faculty for matching the words with exactly the right musical sentiment, and their feeling for verbal accentuation was remarkable in its thoughtfulness and accuracy. They could express every*

[4] "Ballet." *Grove's Dictionary of Music and Musicians.* 1954 ed.

> *kind of mood, whether grave or gay, and their resources were almost unlimited for expressing anything in the nature of realism.*[5]

Composers were clearly not focused on formality but rather on the task at hand, to partner with the greatest poets of their time, to set these beautiful words in powerful ways.

The word *madrigal* unfolds from an international stage. Its origin is from northern Italy, perhaps as early as the 12th century as a song type not parallel to its later 16th century descendent. In 1898 Signor Leandro Bianene, Professor of neo-Latin literature in the University of Pisa, in an essay within *Rassegna bibliographica della letteratura Italiana,* a Pisan magazine, traced the derivation of the word from Latin *matricale,* to the English *madrigal.* By the pairing of words, as *lingua maternal* means "mother tongue," so *carmen matricale,* or *cantus matricalis,* may have stood for "mother song."[6] Flemish composers, who in the early 16th century are now in Italy, Verdelot, Willaert and Arcadelt, inscribe *madrigali* on their title pages.

So the word *madrigal* came to England from Italy (*madrigale)*; but it was actually the Flemish, who brought the modern form to Italy, and they claimed an earlier Englishman, John Dunstable, as an influence. Thus the cause-to-effect here is a full circle. And the cycle is fulfilled when a clerk in the Cathedral of St. Paul, Nicholas Yonge, popularized the Italian madrigal in England by publishing selections from his personal collection of Italian madrigals, adapted to English words, *Musica Transalpina* (1588).

William Byrd curiously did not use the term *madrigal* in his first two sets of secular compositions in 1588 and 1599. Morley's first set of secular pieces was termed *Canzonets* (1593), but when his second set for four voices was called *madrigals* (1594*),* the English for the next forty years generally retained the term.

To draw a concise definition for the word *madrigal* would over-simply our cause here. Within our historical perspective we hold examples of labeling that are inconsistent within usage. The circular cause and effect of the madrigal's national origin again underscores its diverse nature. It is within this context that we pursue our investigation of the English madrigal.

---

[5] Edmund H. Fellowes. *The English Madrigal,* 34-35.

[6] Edmund H. Fellowes. *The English Madrigal,* 26.

History of the Madrigal

The English madrigal is a single coordinate in the nested continuum; it exists as a phenomenal testimony to the unfolding of human expression. The madrigal is a synthesis of independent elements (i.e. poetry and music), compositional craft, Renaissance style, and high Humanist thinking.

For a brief sixty years in England the madrigal held its popularity. William Byrd, from his "Address to the Reader" in his volume of compositions (1588) set the scene for what was to be: "There is not any Musicke of Instruments whatsoever, comparable to that which is made by the voices of Men, where the voices are good, and the same well sorted and ordered." However, it is doubtful that madrigals were much sung after the year 1640. Samuel Pepys, an author and man of refined taste, in his diary (March 10, 1667), described Morley's *Introduction of Musique* as a "very good but unmethodical book." And in another entry (September 15, 1667) he recorded that "after having sung several good things with friends, he (Pepys) was more and more confirmed that singing with many voices is not singing but a sort of instrumental musique, the sense of the words being lost by not being heard, and especially as they set them with Fuges *(sic)* or words, one after another, whereas singing properly, I think, should be put with one or two voices and the counterpoint."[7] Thus the general opinion of this later date was that madrigal singing, and perhaps concerted singing in general, was no longer popular.

> And this, in fact, is the remarkable truth: Byrd, Tallis, Wilbye, Morley, Dowland and Weelkes were all living and in the height of their public success in the year 1600.

During the reign of Queen Elizabeth I the singing of Italian madrigals became a popular household activity. Madrigals were sung essentially as entertainment, to be enjoyed by the household after meals and on special occasions. Alternating between evenings of instrumental consort music and vocal music, the large volume of repertoire exists because of the popularity of the activity. But such music was not available as formal compositions, printed and distributed. Therefore, composers were hired by families to provide these materials for their evening recreation. And for an active period of time (forty to sixty years) madrigal composers of England defined a lasting musical style.

Employing sweet melodies the compositions are nested into a sophisticated imitative craft. Texts by the most celebrated poets of the day are adorned by the best composers of the day. Through the imagination of sound painting, emotions are captured inside the context of modes and harmony. But it must be emphasized that madrigals are built from stylistic details that are shared and common to all from the same time.

These "essentials to the essence"[8] are organic to all musical styles. From earliest monophonic chant to the latest contemporary composition, essentials exist to differentiate styles and periods of music. It is enlightening to chart the length of each

---

[7] Edmund H. Fellowes. *The English Madrigal Composers,* 25.

[8] Coined by the author in 1986 to mean that each musical period and its styles contains differentiated essential elements, which are understood, when integrated by a listener, as musical essence.

large-scale style period and to note the shortening of time between one to the next. The Medieval period spans a timeline from "earliest" to 1450, and this can be subdivided into chant and subsequent polyphony ("earliest" to c. 1000, and 1000 to 1450); the Renaissance period extends from 1450-1600; the Baroque period from 1600-1750; the Classical period is cited as 1750-1820; the Early Romantic period is given as 1820-1850 and the late Romantic period from 1850-1900. As one can see, the length of these periods is decreasing from 1000 years in the early medieval times to from 30 to 50 years in the nineteenth century. Even more telling is that twentieth century styles vary from individual composer to composer rather than from epoch to epoch. Of course, there are isolated examples of short-lived "schools" with a master and select devotees. However, in general we see a distinct compression in the timeline of stylistic lifetimes.

In this context the English madrigal style itself had a limited lifespan from only the late sixteenth century to the early seventeenth century, perhaps at most sixty years. Thomas Morley (1558-1602) was a guiding force in taking its Italian/Flemish model and transforming it into the English madrigal. And the timing was perfect because at the same time that Morley was inspiring other English composers like Farnaby, Farmer, or Bennett and ultimately Kirbye, Weelkes and Wilbye, there were also the great popular sonneteers, Shakespeare and Campion with whom they could collaborate. And this, in fact, is the remarkable truth: Byrd, Tallis, Wilbye, Morley, Dowland and Weelkes were all living and in the height of their public success in the year 1600. Edmund H. Fellowes writes in his book, *The English Madrigal,* "It may be doubted whether any other nation has ever been able to boast of five [he omits one] such great names in a group of contemporary composers."[9]

A choral conductor has many choices of repertoire for building concert programs. Although the English madrigal is distinguished as a quality body of literature, and is available easily through publication, it is also perceived as too "old" or complicated. Such a myth exists because so much of today's music is packaged for convenience, and madrigals require study, and understanding. Hopefully this handbook contributes to each choral conductor, student, or lover of madrigals by providing useful information and guidelines to follow for successful performance. We have approached the madrigal as a marriage of both music and poetry and address both genres with equal attention. For across the wide vista of stylistic practice, nothing contributes to successful performance more than good information.

[9] Edmund H. Fellowes. *The English Madrigal, 25.*

Tactus and Rhythm: Implications on Conducting

Renaissance notation, the madrigal without exception, is comprised of a very active notation--one that implies interactive and multi-dimensional levels-- of the musical material.

> The responsibility of a conductor is to seek to understand the definitions and implications of Renaissance notation, and to communicate these possibilities clearly to the singers in rehearsal.

Effective conducting of Renaissance music is complicated by assumptions and musical memories, which we, products of the end of the twentieth century, bring frequently into our interpretations. Rodney Eichenburger writes, "that in preparing to conduct Renaissance music our twentieth century ears make it difficult not to be highly influenced by the characteristics of all of the intervening stylistic periods." Yes, we acknowledge and promote certain musical elements of the Renaissance while ignoring, and literally misrepresenting, others. Fluctuation of tempo, articulation, intensity, and rhythm are commonly at play in Renaissance music, but we may give attention to only dynamics, or incorrectly deplore syncopation, or falsely minimize the resultant effect of bar-line, accentuation, and the like. To repeat, the conducting of Renaissance music is largely a resultant interaction of musical material, unique to a given composition and its component phrases. The responsibility of a conductor is to seek to understand the definitions and implications of Renaissance notation, and to communicate these possibilities clearly to the singers in rehearsal.

The conductor provides a framework of gesture within which stylistic interactions may function. Meter and *tactus* are foundations of the gesture that build Renaissance phrase. Once the organizational units of meter and *tactus* have been established, patterns of notes become more clearly discernable.

The study of *tactus,* and the practice of *tactus,* to define rhythmic movement in the madrigal are in strong contrast to those who promote agogic word accentuation as the defining rhythmic principle in the Renaissance. Primary-source writings, such as the examples cited in this work, undeniably exist to support *tactus,* but it has been a common practice to refute the existence of metric regularity, to rather focus upon text accent, to construct complex and overlapping rhythms between voice parts. This proves, however, to be inaccurate in practice because it "fills in spaces," with extraneous musical gestures, that do not exist in historic evidence. Such resultant "rebarring" of rhythmic movement adds accentuations, which do not otherwise exist, and more importantly erases the effect of syncopation, undeniably an important expressive element.

Such misunderstandings are the result of two false assumptions. First, that part books did not manifest bar lines, and therefore such regular accentuation did not affect correctly the rhythmic movement. And second, that accentuation is assumed to be always at the front end of a stressed syllable, at the beginning of a given duration.

In the first case it is accepted that manuscript collections were preserved not in full scores, but in sets of individual voice parts. Frequently, several manuscripts were collected into a single part book, but one book only was printed for each vocal part. From extant sources, it seems certain that composers wrote the first draft of a piece in full score, with vertical alignment. But the score was not then used for performance, but rather as the source for the creation of the part books. The full scores were destroyed, believed to have no further usefulness. It is interesting that there was not any value seen in preserving the scores, neither in private collections nor with the sets of part-books. However, the hypothesis that vertical "bar lines" did not exist in the part books is not accurate; they were instead implied. The "books of songs or ayres" of John Dowland are published in a format that further supports our discussion. On the left page the soprano part, with lute accompaniment, includes bar lines, while on the right page the other voice parts are written in part-part fashion, sans bar lines. But clearly bar lines are part of the music.[10]

The second assumption that an agogic accent falls only on the front end of a rhythmic notation, on the front of a stressed syllable, is also not accurate. For, in fact, the stressed point can occur **within** a note's length. For example, any note of duration can be rendered with *messa da voce,* a growth-decay articulation over a single note. The stress is, therefore, inside the noted duration on the climax of the *messa da voce*, not at the front end. This was frequently the manner in which a textual accent would begin at the weak point of a measure, but reach full bloom of accentuation on the fall of the subsequent measure. And therefore, such articulation does not imply a metric shift, but rather syncopation.

However, one of the most frequent mistakes by modern editors is to rebar the music, to reorganize the rhythmic meters and to shift bar lines. This rhythmic shifting, intended to minimize syncopation and maximize smoothness, serves to actually misrepresent the music. It becomes clear, if one examines the part books, that mixed meters would have been impossible; mensuration signs indicated very clearly at the beginning of the piece that a certain note value--usually the *breve* (our modern whole note) in the very early Renaissance and the *semi-breve* (our modern half note) throughout most of the sixteenth and all of the seventeenth century--was specified as the regular metric unit and these were then organized into a defined *tactus*. If no change in mensuration occurred, the metric organization also did not change.

It takes effort for a conductor to access primary sources, however editions of these theoretical writings exist in most research libraries, and in fact offer valuable insights into important performance guidelines. In order to better understand the expression of syncopation we need to examine *tactus* and syncopation from some of these available sources.

On the subject of *tactus,* Johannes Cochlaeus asked in his treatise, *Tetrachordum Musices* (1511), "What is mensural tactus?" He answers, "It is a continuous movement maintained in a given measurement, for time is recognized by movement, and also the temporal duration of a tone."[11]

Sebald Heyden in his treatise, *De Arte Canendi* (1540) also asked the question, "What is tactus?" He writes, "It is a movement or stroking motion of a finger fitting the value of all notes and rests into an equally divided temporal beat. The tactus therefore defines very accurately the temporal value of every note and rest. Moreover, nothing definite can be understood or taught about the length, perfection, imperfection,

---

[10] Original editions of both the first (1597) and third (1603) books of "Songs or Ayres" by John Dowland, printed by Peter Short, were examined in the rare book collection of the Huntington Library (San Marino, CA).

[11] *American Institute of Musicology,* 1978, no. 23, 68.

augmentation and diminution of notes unless previously the tactus has been definitely established."[12]

And Tomas de Santa Maria in his *Arte de tañer fantasia* (1565) records, "All tactus are measured and regulated by the length of the first tactus, that is, that the amount of time occupied by the first tactus be occupied by each of the ones that follow, so that no more time elapses in one than in the other."[13]

The *tactus* serves therefore as the accepted organizational practice for the movement of music during the time of English madrigals. Such regularity of movement, as well as rhetorical devices, namely syncopation, was the building block of expression. But it was also certain that a *tactus* has feel, that it is virtually impossible to not leave a mark of distinction when moving from *tactus* to *tactus*. The sense of *tactus* regularity is present despite any intention to move smoothly between *tacti,* or to otherwise create an artificial equality in stress. The regularity is desired, and in fact is what allows rhetorical devices to function.

By keeping the metric structure regular, or invariable, syncopation works as an exception against regular meter. In other words there is, to quote Dr. Dennis Shrock (University of Oklahoma), "a frequent expressive opposition to the regular metric organization." But contrary, when the solution is to rebar the music, the metric opposition is falsely aligned with the musical material and the syncopation ceases to be recognized. Many treatises of the time refer to the importance of syncopation. Quoting again from Sebald Heyden in his *De Arte Canendi* (1540):

> *Syncopation is generally considered to occur whenever the mensural values of semibreves are sung for some time in opposition to the uniform movement of the tactus. Our brief advice here concerning this disparity is as follows. While singing, do not allow the note values to return to agreement with the tactus, but persist vigorously in the disparity until the notes are reconciled to the tactus, for such a disparity hardly ever extends beyond the second or third tempus.*

In *L'antica Musica* (1555) Nicola Vicentino writes, "If syncopation is employed in all voice parts simultaneously, it will not sound like a syncopation, since syncopation can be perceived only if at least one part sings on the downbeat, while the others sing on the upbeat."

And Thomas Morley writes this statement in his *A Plain and Easy Introduction to Practical Music* (1597); "A cadence must always be bound or then odd, driving a small note through a greater, which the Latins and those who have of late days written the art of music call 'syncopation,' for all binding and hanging upon notes is called syncopation."

The modern term "conductor" is derived from the Latin *conducere,* "to lead or to guide." However, this is not what was understood at the time of the English madrigal. The conductor of Renaissance music should show a clear *tactus,* in either simple or compound meter, as called for by the proportional signs of the musical score. Down-up for simple; down-down-up for compound. It is more beneficial in rehearsal to refer to

---

[12] *American Institute of Musicology,* 1972, no. 26, 53.

[13] Charles Jacobs, *Tempo Notation in Renaissance Spain.* Brooklyn: Institute of Medieval Music, 1964, 7.

the "up" gesture as "**ready**," since this better captures the kinesthetic language of music, specifically "anacrusis." At the very least the language of direction and kinesthetic better capture the intention of the *tactus* than do numbers, 1-2 or 1-2-3. Therefore, it is more productive to articulate the *tactus* as either "down-ready" for duple time, or "down-down-ready" for triple time.

The most common illustration of the gesture of *tactus* is that of placing one's hand on a tabletop. "Down-ready" is the motion of touching the hand down gently on the table and then lifting the hand in preparation to touch again. "Down-down-ready" is to touch one's hand on the table, and rest the hand for an additional pulse before lifting the hand in preparation for the next "down." Therefore, "down-down" is not a continuous motion in a fall, but rather resting for the second pulse.

> The craft of imagery best defines the madrigal, and imagery was achieved with consummate imagination.

When compared to the continuous motion inherent in modern conducting "patterns" *tactus* is experienced as a framework rather than a meter, a kinesthetic rather than an action. And the kinesthetic quality of *tactus* is different from that of "pattern." *Tactus* is ruled by *crusis* and *anacrusis,* by touch and preparation.

Let's summarize. Within the *tactus* there is little "filling in," with extraneous gesture, of the internal time between kinesthetic movements. *Tactus* is the source of control without itself being controlling, the source of structure, not detail. Musical feel becomes the regular metrical organization of each madrigal. Singers are trained, are guided by gesture through syncopation by a conductor, who facilitates the beginning and ending of events--rather than being an independent element from the music itself, or the interpretation itself.

Johann Matteson (1681-1764) wrote in *Der Volkommene Kappellmeister*, "The keeping of the beat is to speak the principle function of the director of a piece of music at its presentation. . . . what to think of the useless stamping, din and pounding with sticks, keys and feet. . . a little sign, not only with the hand but merely with the eyes and gestures, could accomplish most. . .if only the performers would assiduously keep their eyes on the director."

Tomas de Santa Maria in his treatise, *Libro llamado de tañer fantasia* (1565) wrote this narrative:

> *There are two different ways of beating (time) in practical music. In the first one the measure (as it has been said) is divided and alsoseparated into two equal parts. This is the measurement of proportion which is also known by the name of Ternario, in which, in the three parts of which it is composed, the first two are spent on the down-beat, and the other one in the up-beat; this is done by singing two semi-breves in the down-beat, and one in the up-beat. Four things are required for making perfect measure. The first is to make the down-beat and up-beat with the hand, without spending (as it has been said) more time from the down to the up-beat than from the up to the down-beat, and although the up-beat as (well as) the down-beat has no point at which to stop, it should nevertheless be made as if it would stop or mark something, for frequently we see the beat being made loosely without stopping the hand*

> *up or down; thus the hand must make as if it were striking above and below. Each time has two beats. The second thing is, that when the hand makes the down-beat, it should stay quiet during the time that the half-measure lasts, without lowering it to the point where it should make the down-beat, and for this it is necessary to raise and lower the hand equally and evenly, that is, not to have more speed of movement going up than going down.*

Writing about music has never been a simple task.

Stylistic Expression

Madrigal texts were drawn from a supply of first-rate poetry. The names of those who wrote the words are largely not known, never recorded in the part books. But some are identified because the same poems exist in other sources as well. And they are contemporaries of William Shakespeare, like Edmund Spenser, Ben Jonson, Christopher Marlowe, Thomas Campion, John Donne, Walter Raleigh, all during the Golden Age of English literature.

Although it is from such literature that the English madrigalists drew their inspiration, expression is not unique or even germane to the English madrigal, but rather was built upon the earlier inventiveness of Josquin des Pres (1450-1521), Clement Jannequin (1485-1558), and perhaps even as early as the unknown composers of chant.[14] Elizabethans did not invent the wheel of imagery; they used it. And they developed the sensibility of madrigalism to the height of its form.

The madrigal is defined by its imagery, and imagery was achieved with consummate vividness. The composers were masters of composition and capitalized partly on the fact that this was the high point in history of Renaissance counterpoint, both sacred and secular. The madrigalist dealt with poetry generally phrase-by-phrase, line-by-line. One line may be the source of point-of-imitation technique, while the next may be treated homo-rhythmically. The plan of the composition may take on several large sections, each section articulated by either new musical material or a returning "hook." But the composer was always striving to set the poem with a sense of cohesion and symmetry of design.

---

[14] M. Clement Morin, Dean Emeritus of the Faculty of Music at the University of Montreal, wrote an essay "Gregorian Musical Words" in *Choral Essays: A Tribute to Roger Wagner,* ed. William Belan (Thomas House, 1993). He develops his thesis that madrigalism was a common practice in Gregorian chant, and identifies recurring melodic patterns that adorn scriptural text of Rejoice, *Cross and Glory, Ave-Hail, Kaire, Lasting melos, Tone-painting, Madrigalism, and Musical Exegesis.*

Reading Texts and Hearing the Poet's Music

English professors seldom talk about "music" when they teach poetry, and choral directors seldom talk about "text" and poetics when teaching and training singers and other conductors to perform madrigals or other poetic texts set to music. This is not to discount the many teachers with dual expertise or those who take a consciously interdisciplinary approach to their instruction. Rather, the observation arises from the shared experience of the authors of this volume, in their 35 combined years of university instruction. We have discovered that music and text, so intertwined and unified in Western European cultural history, have become sadly estranged in the modern classroom, victims of the division of departments into English and Music, as if the disciplines were not often one and the same, particularly in the Golden Age of the English Madrigal. We want to encourage the "marriage" of music and text and reveal the profit and joys of thinking about text and music together and not as separate academic domains or as separate arts, in relation to study and also to performance.

In interviewing choral performers about the English madrigal, some of whom have been performing choral music for 20 years (and many of them conductors themselves) one learns, surprisingly, that the nearly sole focus is on notes, time, and syllables with no larger awareness or concern for what literary critics would call "meaning" beyond the superficial subject matter of the text. For example, they apprehend that a text was perhaps about love and kissing, and they recognize the pastoral setting of texts such as "Fair Phyllis" or "Sweet Amaryllis" but were so, and rightly, occupied with their parts that they simply had no time to consider the purely textual universe separate from the music. Therefore, a separate chapter, hopefully not too pedantic, on symbol, metaphor, end-stops, enjambment, and meter is needed in order to show the poetic arts that may not be commonly perceived as central to the performance of madrigals, even though they form the very basic poetic structure upon which any musical setting must, by definition, be based.[15]

---

[15] For the kind of study and practice I am here recounting and recommending, several brief yet full and effective overviews of English prosody are available, particularly in popular poetry anthologies, such as the *Norton Introduction to Poetry, Shorter Fourth Edition*, ed Margaret Ferguson et al. (New York: Norton), 1103-22; For a concise glossary of literary terms, see, among many others, *250 Poems: A Portable Anthology*, ed. Peter Schakel and Jack Ridl (Boston and New York: Bedford/St. Martins), 381-95. Two 20th-century books on the madrigal contain particularly noteworthy chapters on "text"; see "The Madrigal Lyrics" in Edmund Horace Fellows, *The English Madrigal Composers*, (London: Oxford), 19XX, pp. 140-157, and "The Works" in Fellowe's *The English Madrigal* (London: Oxford), 1925 pp. 64-80. For modern authoritative overviews of English prosody see Elizabeth Couper-Kuhlen, *An Introduction to English Prosody* (Tübingen: M. Niemeyer), 1986, and Burton Raffel, *From Stress to Stress: an Autobiography of English Prosody* (Hamden, Conn.: Archon Books), 1992. For those interested in exploring the larger history of literary criticism and critical theory, spanning the Classical theories of Plato and Aristotle, through Elizabethan attitudes codified in Sir Phillip Sidney's *Apology for Poetry*, and up to the various schools of contemporary thought see *The Critical Tradition: Classic Texts and Contemporary Trends*, ed. David H. Richter (Boston and New York: Bedford/St. Martins), 1998.

> If composers paint with sound to create drama, movement, emotion, conflict, and resolutions, so do poets, through the use of literary devices.

We have found that an awareness of text and poetics can dramatically enhance the conductors' and the performers' appreciation of their art, allowing them to hear the craft, the beauty, and the profound "music" of written texts, completely apart from the musical score to which they might be set. Also, since many poetic texts are not set to music by the same author, the texts are not necessarily designed to rely on setting but on their own internal dynamic, which must be learned and studied. For example, Monteverdi set the poems of Petrarch, who wrote and died 150 years before hand, with no awareness, obviously, of how his words would be rendered by this unborn, though fellow Italian, composer. Petrarch gave his poems their own music, as did Shakespeare, who also wrote actual song texts, to be performed with music on the stage, within his plays. Other poets, of course, such as Campion, wrote both words and music. But whether the text is written independent of the music or strictly for the musical setting, knowledge of poetic craft can profoundly deepen the understanding, appreciation, and performance of song.

If composers paint with sound to create drama, movement, emotion, conflict, and resolution, so do poets, through the use of literary devices. Through formal instruction, the goal is to sensitize conductors and singers to the poet's craft, so that they can see and hear what the composer is building upon, what complex drama he is exposing, exploiting, and rendering into sound.[16] When the audience, for its part, is also involved in the process, through hearing a recitation and critical analysis before the performance, it becomes familiar with the landscape of the texts, the sonic power of the verse, its tempo, rhythm, volume, tone, and meaning. This creates a strong sense of anticipation for the sung performance that follows. The hearers also become invested in the emotional drama of the poetry and thus listen anxiously for the musical unfolding of what they have just heard poetically. This intensifies the aesthetic fulfillment of the members of the audience and also deepens their knowledge of the composer's and of the conductor's craft, as they attend to every sonic decision the composer has made in depicting, literally "making a picture of" the poetic narrative of the text.

---

[16] Any time is a good time to cite the great Modern American poet, Ezra Pound: "Literature is language charged with meaning," *ABC of Reading* (New York: New Directions), 1960, p. 28. Though it has fallen out of classroom use, Pound's *ABC of Reading* still repays study and provides an overview of the processes of meaningful analytic engagement with literary texts, with particular focus on the English lyric.

Samples of English Prosody

The texts from two very famous Renaissance sonnets will exemplify the poetic musicality we have been discussing. These texts were not written to be set musically and for that reason they serve as excellent case studies in the classroom when introducing conductors and singers to purely poetic musicality. We intend that the sensitivity and knowledge gained in examining these sonnets, or any of a thousand other like them, can be transferred over to the performance of specific madrigal texts in the English tradition. Madrigals such as "Faire Phyllis" and "The Silver Swan" (examined in detail in this volume, see pages 26-42) are often brief and deceptively simple but operate according to the same poetic principles as the great Elizabethan sonnets. They use meter, verse form, rhythm, tempo, and rhyme to create music before a note is ever composed or sung.

Let us consider the text of one of Edmund Spenser's *Amoretti*, or little love poems, a sonnet sequence that traces the courtship and eventual marriage of the poet and his lover:

Sonnet #75

One day I wrote her name upon the strand,
But came the waves and washed it away:
Agayne I wrote it with a second hand,
But came the tyde, and made my paynes his pray.
Vayne man, sayd she, that doest in vaine assay,
A mortall thing so to immortalize.
For I my selve shall lyke to this decay,
And eek my name bee wiped out lykewize.

Not so, (quod I) let baser things devize,
To dy in dust, but you shall live by fame:
My verse your virtues rare shall eternize,
And in the havens wryte your glorious name:
Where whenas death shall all the world subdew,
Our love shall live, and later life renew.[17]

When presenting a poem like this to conductors and singers who are not "English majors" and who do not need to become expert in the particulars of contemporary literary theory or historical analysis, one can benefit from an early 20th-century method of reading called "New Criticism," though now it is considered by some (erroneously) to be old and outdated.[18] New Criticism sees the poem as an artful world unto itself, a little universe

---

[17] Spenser's and Shakespeare's sonnet sequence is available, whole or in part, in any number of anthologies and in Spenser's collected works, in addition to full texts available on line. The versions cited here are from, respectively, *English Sixteenth-Century Verse*, ed. Richard S. Sylvester (New York and London: Norton), p. 382, and *Shakespeare's Sonnets*, ed. Douglas Bush and Alfred Harbage (Baltimore: Penguin), 1961, p. 93.

[18] For an extended example of a close critical reading, including a defense of the English professor's traditional art, see the chapter "Yet Once More," Stanley

of structure, tension, opposition, and dramatic movement. A larger-scale critical application might engage theoretical or historical aspects of the poem. For example, a feminist analysis that focuses on the power of the woman's voice can be interesting and important, particularly when confronting male-authored texts. Generally, however, it is best to begin with an isolated consideration of the basic setting, scene, sound, and sense of the poem.

What is Spenser's poem about? Most basically, it recounts a man's story about his attempt to write a woman's name on the sand:

(1) One day I wrote her name upon the strand, (a)
(2) But came the waves and washed it away: (b)
(3) Agayne I wrote it with a second hand, (a)
(4) But came the tyde, and made my paynes his pray. (b)

followed by her response;

(5) Vayne man, sayd she, that doest in vaine assay, (b)
(6) A mortall thing so to immortalize. (c)
(7) For I my selve shall lyke to this decay, (b)
(8) And eek my name bee wiped out lykewize. (c)

then his response to her.

(9) Not so, (quod I) let baser things devize, (c)
(10) To dy in dust, but you shall live by fame: (d)
(11) My verse your virtues rare shall eternize, (c)
(12) And in the havens wryte your glorious name: (d)
(13) Where whenas death shall all the world subdew, (e)
(14) Our love shall live, and later life renew. (e)

We are not going to be confused by the image of lovers writing their names, or initials in the sand, whether the poet mentions a heart with an arrow through it or not. We are off to a good start.

With the basic drama of the poem demystified in this way, we are ready to look at the particular craft involved. The text is not in prose but in a structured verse form with a particular meter. Each component contributes to the text's larger meaning. "Verse form," relates to the poem's structure, the number of lines, the use of rhyme, and the relationship of the stanzas. "Meter" relates to the rhythm of the individual feet, which are the basic units of composition, defined by where the stress or emphasis falls. The most common meter in the English tradition is *iambic*, in which a foot is made up of an unstressed syllable followed by a stressed one; "One **day** I **wrote** her **name** up**on** the **strand**" is a sequence of five iambic feet, with stress on the following syllables, marked in bold: "day," "wrote," "name," "-on," "strand." Some theorists say this echoes the human heartbeat, but in any case it is the primary meter of Chaucer, Shakespeare, Milton, Spenser and all the great poets from then to modern times. Because there are five feet

---

Fish's analysis of Milton's "Lycidas" in *Professional Correctness: Literary Study and Political Change* (Oxford: Clarendon), 1995, pp. 1-17.

of iambs, we call this meter "iambic pentameter;" if the line were three feet, it would be "tri-meter;" if four feet, "tetrameter;" if six, "hexameter." To poets, the iambic pentameter is the equivalent of "common time" in music. But very few poems rely on the constant repetition of iambic feet, and a reversal of the iamb called a *trochee* (a stressed then unstressed syllable), for the use of a *spondee* (two consecutive stresses) vary and enliven the poem for dramatic, sonic, rhythmic, and emotional effect.

Moving from the line to the stanza, to discern the over-all rhyme scheme that binds the poem, we mark the rhyming words with letters in the margins: "strand" is an "a" since it is the first word in the scheme, and "away," which does not rhyme with "strand," is "b." "Hand" perks up the reader as a rhyme with "strand," and so it merits another "a." "Prey" reconnects us to "away" and gets a "b" resulting in "abab" a very popular, viable sonnet stanza form. This group of four lines, bound by this rhyme scheme is called a *quatrain*, the first building block of the sonnet, in this case a "Spenserian sonnet." Readers of Petrarch, Shakespeare, and Sidney will find other rhyme schemes as the defining marks of these sonneteers.

If we continue the process through the other quatrains, we will see that the scheme proceeds as such: stanza two with "assay" starts with another "b" like "prey" from stanza one, but then it introduces a new sound "ize" in "immortalize" and "likewise." This new sound we must call "c," creating in the second stanza "bcbc." Notice that this pattern is not independent from that of the first quatrain, since the two quatrains are linked and interlaced by the b-rhyme. Continuing this logic, the third quatrain starts with the last sound from the previous one, with "devise" beginning the pattern "cdcd" with the new sound of "fame" and "name" marked by "d." The poem thus builds upon itself while moving dramatically forward by the constant introduction of new sounds, as the adventure on the beach between the man and woman evolves. The scheme is tightly wrought—not an inappropriate structure for a dialogic poem about love, time, continuity, and connectedness.

I have called these three sections quatrains, but also one must consider the relations of the first eight lines of the sonnet (*octave*) to the rest of the poem, the (*sestet*). Musicians, of course, should have no trouble with these terms. Two structures exist at once: 4+4+4+2 and 8+6. Conductors might reflect that this tension, at least impressionistically, compares to "2 against 3" or other time signatures in music. In this poem, the octave includes the dialogue between the lovers (the first quatrain is his, the second hers), while the entire sestet is taken up with the poet's response, culminating in the thunderous final couplet.

This sound in "subdue" and "renew" we call "e." This couplet is, of course, part of the sestet, but it is separated from the third quatrain, as it is in all English sonnets, by its rhyme and confined syntax. It is very much a separate sentence, though still in the man's voice. A couplet is like a *coda*, bringing the poem (not always but certainly in this case) to dramatic conclusion, resolution, resolve, or determination. The subject of the poem has been how love can overcome time—no mere walk on the beach—and the male poet ends with a pledge that their love will live forever, if not in the sand then in the verses he composes about her, which no wave can wash away.

The next thing to consider is how the particular composition of the poem, foot by foot, contributes to this theme of the eternal power of art and love. Let's consider the iambic pentameter; the entire first quatrain is regular, with strict iambic feet (the pentameter itself seldom if ever changes in sonnet form). The poet is attempting, in a stout, stalwart, workaday fashion, to hammer out his hopes on the beach, with the waves just as matter of factly coming to wash his labor away. The reliability, the inevitability, the constancy of wave and water are reflected in the unvarying thump of the iambic feet. This is regularity put to good thematic use.

(1) One day I wrote her name upon the strand, (a)
(2) But came the waves and washed it away: (b)
(3) Agayne I wrote it with a second hand, (a)
(4) But came the tyde, and made my paynes his prey. (b)

The regularity is ruptured by the woman's voice in line five with the explosive spondee "vain man," followed in the rest of the line by four feet of calming iambs. The spondee is a shout, a reprimand, and a symbol clash against the foolish plodding of the silly poet. Her meter then reverts to consistent iambs until the end of her quatrain.

(5) Vayne man, sayd she, that doest in vaine assay, (b)
(6) A mortall thing so to immortalize. (c)
(7) For I my selve shall lyke to this decay, (b)
(8) And eek my name bee wiped out lykewize. (c)

With the spondee "not so," the poet himself returns in full vigor, paralleling the effect of "vain man" above. The exclamation defends his position, which he elaborates in fairly consistent iambs for the rest of the poem. The variation from iambic verse is scant but very powerful and meaningful, emphasizing the dramatic point of contention between the two lovers, who really function as adversaries in their attitudes toward immortality. But the poem is, finally, a love poem, and the couplet that ends the sonnet promises that poetry and love will overcome fate, time, and death.

If read well, this poem should, without any consideration of musical setting, make us hear the waves as they pound out eternity upon the shore. One should also hear the music of defiance and of eternal hope in the poet's constant, "eternalizing," "immortalizing" song. At this point, after this type of close rhythmic and thematic analysis, it is a good exercise to imagine setting the text to music, exploring and expanding the conflicts, tensions, and resolution that occur in the seaside narrative. How might one paint particular lines and words? How might the structural tensions and progressions of the sonnet's structure be expressed? How can we render the triumphant final couplet—if we even agree that the couplet is triumphant? It is always possible to hear doubt and anxiety, even when the surface letter of the text would seem to deny them.

(9) Not so, (quod I) let baser things devize, (c)
(10) To dy in dust, but you shall live by fame: (d)
(11) My verse your virtues rare shall eternize, (c)
(12) And in the havens wryte your glorious name: (d)
(13) Where whenas death shall all the world subdew, (e)
(14) Our love shall live, and later life renew. (e)

Which brings us conveniently to our next selection, a poem from the greatest English sonneteer, William Shakespeare, who here depicts a relationship somewhat reminiscent of Spenser's but with significant thematic and rhythmic variations.

Sonnet #71

No longer mourn for me when I am dead
Than you shall hear the surly sullen bell
Give warning to the world that I am fled
From this vile world, with vilest worms to dwell.
Nay, if you read this line, remember not
That hand that writ it, for I love you so
That I in your sweet thoughts would be forgot
If thinking on me then should make you woe.
O, if, I say, you look upon this verse
When I, perhaps, compounded am with clay,
Do not so much as my poor name rehearse,
But let your love even with my life decay,
  Lest the wise world should look into your moan
  And mock you with me after I am gone.

A basic overview of the poem—always our starting place—shows us that the poet is speaking to a friend or lover, asking him/her not to mourn when he dies. The themes of death and love between two people recall Spenser's sonnet, but this poem is not a dialogue; one speaker conducts the entire discourse. This invites us to look into the psychology of this speaker; why does he not want to be mourned? Why is he even thinking of dying? What is his tone? Is he perhaps self-pitying? Does he actually want to be mourned, perhaps seeking the very *opposite* of his request? The element of manipulation and even neurosis enters into our consideration.

> There are no accidents in the music of the text. But readers, singers, and hearers throughout time will see, hear, recite, and sing the words in different ways, depending of their particular apprehension of what is going on sonically in the poems.

A larger apprehension of Shakespeare's sequence would tell us that this poem is written not to a woman but to a young man whom the poet has been commissioned to write poetry for, encouraging him to marry. But as the sequence progresses, the poet has become emotionally involved with the young man, making the poet self-conscious of his age and eventual demise, in this "May-December" male relationship. This context is helpful, but even without it, we can see the themes of death, age, self-pity, and anxiety in the very texture and craft of the sonnet.

A quick look at the rhyme scheme shows that it differs from Spenser's, with each quatrain having a discrete pattern. The pattern that obtains is distinctly Shakespearean: abab cdcd efef gg. This divides the poem into three bursts of emotion and exhortation, three injunctions, three dramatic images that build to the complex, bitter, final couplet, which merges hatred for the world with a protective love of the young man. The older poet does not want his beloved to suffer the shame of showing his love for the dead poet, whom the rest of the world, for unexplained reasons, despises.

Turning to quatrain one, we hear something quite different from what we heard in Spenser. The entire quatrain is "enjambed;" that is, the syntax of each line does not conclude at the end of the written verse, forcing the reader to continue rapidly to the next line to find syntactic meaning. Put another way, you cannot stop at the end of the line because if you do you will be left hanging waiting for meaning to occur.

(1) No longer mourn for me when I am dead (a)
(2) Than you shall hear the surly sullen bell (b)
(3) Give warning to the world that I am fled (a)
(4) From this vile world, with vilest worms to dwell. (b)

The history of the punctuation of the sonnets is murky, since the poet never authorized any formal arrangement. But modern editors usually give the reader a sense of what lines are enjambed and which are "end-stopped," the name we give to lines where the meaning is complete and the mind and voice can "stop" at the end of the line. Most often this is represented by a period or a semicolon, though a comma introducing a coordinating conjunction can create an end stop, as in lines 1-2 and 2-3 of Spenser's poem. Compare the opening lines of each poem to understand the difference between end-stopped and enjambed lines. "One day I wrote her name upon the strand:" this line can stand alone as a complete sentence; it continues but does not grammatically depend on the following line. This makes the reader "stop" longer at line's end, and if we were to progress through Spenser's poem we would see that each line is end-stopped, contributing to the regular rhythm we discussed above, simulating the sound of the tide, which can be heard to progress in a series of stops and restarts.

But Shakespeare's line "No longer mourn for me when I am dead" grammatically depends on the next adverbial phrase, "Than you shall hear the surly sullen bell," specifying what "no longer" in line one means. Don't mourn for me any longer than the death knell tolls. Likewise, line two ends with a subject "surly sullen bell" that needs a verb that only arrives in the next line, "give warning to the world than I am fled." Finally, "fled" at the end of line three depends on the prepositional phrase in line four that tells us the poet has fled, "from this vile world." The quatrain finally ends with the phrase "with vilest worms to dwell." Shakespeare keeps the action moving until we are deep in the grave with the poet, at the great mother of all end stops, death itself, and so the sentence and the music finally come to rest here. The stop at the end of the quatrain and the completion of the first rhyming pattern makes us meditate on the poet's wish. He wants only minimal pity, a short mourning period, and yet he slathers on the pathetic imagery of funeral and death–the sullen bell, the vilest worms, images that compel the very pity that he so passionately forbids. The rapid, near rambling quatrain reveals thus a prickly, self dramatizing, even perhaps neurotic, consciousness. This is not merely a psycho-analytic analysis but a rhetorical, metrical one. The real "mind" of the poet is off limits for us, but his language is not, and it is in this language the manic music of love, aging, and anxiety is being conducted.

The hasty pace continues in the next quatrain with three more enjambed lines, with the end stop postponed until it comes powerfully with the word "woe."

(5) Nay, if you read this line, remember not (c)
(6) That hand that writ it, for I love you so (d)
(7) That I in your sweet thoughts would be forgot (c)
(8) If thinking on me then should make you woe. (d)

The topic of this quatrain is the poet's forbidding mourning, but it focuses not on the grave, as in the first quatrain, but on the pen, on the poet's art that lives on beyond him and has, of course, created the very poem we read. Remember the lines, says Shakespeare, but not the hand that wrote them, since that will make you sad. The irony, of course, is that it is not possible for the young man to separate the two, and thus the quatrain forbids the lamentation that the poet most eagerly seeks. The opening of line five is most likely a spondee (Nay, if), with emphasis on both "Nay" and "if," though one could argue that "if" receives less stress, making the foot potentially a trochee (Nay, if). However, if "if" sounds like it wants to burst out of the line loudly, as a dramatic note of contingency, then we would want to read it with definite stress.

A point is to be made here, which I have intentionally delayed: though the poet is in control of every sound, he does not formally encode specific feet into the poem, as if in a musical score, allowing, rather, for varieties in sonic performance. This does not mean that "anything goes," for the natural phrasal stress of the words prevents too much subjective adventurism: you would not stress the first syllable, for example, of words like "rehearse" or "decay" because that violates the natural stress of those words. In class or rehearsal students should read aloud or work in pairs and mark the text with their impressions of where stress lies. It is likely that most readers will hear the stress and emphasis of both "Nay" and "if," and the more these words are stressed, the more we realize that the poet is hoping passionately for the opposite of what he requests, that is, for "yes" and "when."

The "Oh, if" in line 9, like the opening of line 5, introduces the quatrain with an emphatic spondee, followed by four lines that seem to say little more than the first eight.

(9) O, if, I say, you look upon this verse (e)
(10) When I, perhaps, compounded am with clay, (f)
(11) Do not so much as my poor name rehearse, (e)
(12) But let your love even with my life decay, (f)

We can, in fact, turn Shakespeare's famous quotation from *Hamlet* against him and say that the poet "protests too much;" he wants nothing more than for the young man to think of him each time he reads his poem, not only when the poet is "compounded with clay" but here and now so that the poet can enjoy the love that his mock-tragic verse has inspired.

The final couplet employs a wonderful irony in "wise," for Shakespeare does not really consider a world that would mock him after death to be very wise.

(13) Lest the wise world should look into your moan (g)
(14) And mock you with me after I am gone. (g)

Fearing that the young man will absorb the shame of mourning publicly for such a wretch, Shakespeare tries to protect him from the humiliation of association. "Moan" and "gone" do not rhyme today, but they rhyme well in Elizabethan English, with a long and open "O" vowel (IPA ɑ) in "moan," (as in present day English "caught") creating a groaning rhyme in this final, pitiful plea. Note that "lest the" is a trochee, adding ironic emphasis to the fearful word "lest," followed by regular iambic meter until the end of the poem. The final effect of the couplet is that the young man should now feel protective and defensive of the dying poet and be proud to feel and to display his love for the poet. The sonnet is, finally, an exercise in reverse psychology.

As another exercise, look at all the rhyming words, which take emphasis whether enjambed or not, for they tell the entire story of the poem, betraying the themes of writing, death, and sorrow.

The reaction of some to this analysis might be, "wow, where did you get all that?" Many kinds of meaning and feeling can be ascertained from a reading of the text if, and I emphasize "if," you can point to formal features of the text that support your analysis. These formal features include word choice, imagery, tone, and particularly for our purposes, the pace, rhythm, and sonic emphasis, established by the individual feet and by Shakespeare's extreme use of enjambment. These two examples have been chosen from Spenser and Shakespeare for their importance in literary history, for their proximity to the great Golden Age of madrigals, and for their complex beauty. It is hoped that choral conductors and performers will be able to reproduce infinitely what is modeled here with only two poems. When approaching other sonnets, madrigal texts, or any verses to be studied, whether they are set to music or not, go slowly, look up difficult words, and listen to the sound of each "measure" (which we call "feet") and to the pace, tone, and rhythm of the lines, stanzas, and couplets. There are no accidents in the music of the text. But readers, singers, and hearers throughout time will see, hear, recite, and sing the words in different ways, depending of their particular apprehension of what is going on sonically in the poems. Composers, for their part, when setting texts to music, will choose to dramatize and to paint various features of the written text, depending upon how they have interpreted the written text before them. The more we all listen to the music of the text and the more we explore the intricacies of the marriage between text and music, the richer will be all our experiences as artists in the world of story and song.

At the risk of over-simplifying the process of literary analysis, and its subsequent pursuit of "meaning," a brief summary of the steps recommended above may by helpful:

1) What is the poem about? Begin to demystify the poem with an isolated consideration of the basic setting, scene, sound and sense of the text;
2) Analyze the craft. How many lines? What is the poetic rhythm? How to the stanzas relate to one another? Graph the rhythm scheme, the poetic feet/meter, and regular to irregular word stresses;
3) Consider how the particular composition of the text, foot by foot, contributes to the poem's overall theme. This is the aesthetic part of our understanding, a playful mental game of speculation and imagination. Although there is no absolute right or wrong here, we tend to seek a sense of right**ness** to our interpretation.

Selecting An Edition

When faced with the selection of a madrigal for performance, the selection of a responsible performance edition becomes an important issue. In the best of worlds, editions of early music exist to make important studies of repertoire available to modern performers, not as a vehicle for personal interpretive opinion.

We note there are several areas of scholarship that determine the value of an edition. Available publications, which give us an accurate transcription of primary source manuscript, are important. This means that the transcription from part books must be accurate, that meter and text underlay are accurate.

Again, beware of editorial tampering, where frequent changes of meter have been added to avoid syncopation, or when expressive dynamic and tempo marks are imposed to excess. The best editions allow conductor and singers to make their own informed decisions without the clutter of opinion. Cosmetically, fine editions are presented with clean typesetting, clear text, and an *incipit* that records the original meter, clefs, and note values. The best service an editor can provide is an accurate transcribed score with no additional distractions. Look for helpful performance notes in the front material that give advice on style and practice.

Selected Example #1: Suggestions for Preparation and Performance
***Fair Phyllis* (John Farmer 1599), ed. William Belan with special contributions by Michael Calabrese**
***Gentry Publications*, Catalogue No. JG2369**

Fair Phyllis I saw sitting all alone,
Feeding her flock near to the mountainside.
The shepherds knew not whither she was gone,
But after her lover Amyntas hied.
Up and down he wandered whilst she was missing;
When he found her, O then they fell a kissing.

FAIR PHYLLIS I SAW

JOHN FARMER (c1570-c1605)
Edited by
WILLIAM BELAN

*The keyboard part is not a reduction of the vocal lines, but rather an idiomatic realization for aid in the learning process.

8 2. 9 10
side. The shep - herds knew not, they knew not whith - er she was
side. The shep - herds knew not whith - er she was
side. The shep - herds
side. The
2.
11 12 13
gone, But af - ter her lov -
gone, But af - ter her lov - er,
knew not, they knew not whith - er she was gone, But af - ter her
shep - herds knew not whith - er she was gone, But af - ter

14
15
16
17
- er, her lov - er, but af - ter her lov - er A - myn - tas
— her lov - er, but af - ter her lov - er A - myn - tas
lov - er, her lov - er, but af - ter her lov-er A - myn - tas
her lov - er, but af - ter her lov-er A - myn - tas
18
19
20
hied, Up and down he wan - dered,
hied. Up and down, up and down he
hied. Up and down he wan - dered, up and down, up and
hied. Up and down he wan - dered, he

21
22
23
up and down he wan - dered, up and
wan - dered, up and down he wan - dered, up
down he wan - dered, up and down he wan - dered,
wan - dered, up
24
25
26
down he wan - dered, up and down he wan - dered, up and down
— and down he wan - dered, up and down he wan -
up and down he wan - dered, up and down he wan - dered,
and down he

27
28
29
30
he wan - dered, whilst she was miss - ing; When
dered, he wan - dered, whilst she was miss - ing; When
up and down he wan - dered, whilst she was miss - ing; When
wan - dered, whilst she was miss - ing; When
Tactus
31
32
33
34
he found her,
he found her, O, then they fell a -
he found her, O, then they fell a -
he found her, O, then they fell a -

35
36
37
38 simile
39
O, then they fell a - kiss - ing, a - kiss - ing, O,
kiss - ing, O, then they fell a - kiss - ing, a - kiss - ing, O,
kiss - ing, O, then they fell a - kiss - ing, a - kiss - ing, O,
kiss - ing, O, then they fell a - kiss - ing, a kiss - ing, O,
40
41
42
43
1.
to ms. 19
2.
then they fell a - kiss - ing, kiss - ing.
then they fell a - kiss - ing, kiss - ing.
then they fell a - kiss-ing, up and down he kiss - ing.
then they fell a - kiss - ing, up and kiss - ing.
1.
to ms. 19
2.

Fair Phyllis I saw sitting all alone,
Feeding her flock near to the mountainside.
The shepherds knew not whither she was gone,
But after her lover Amyntas hied.
Up and down he wandered whilst she was missing;
When he found her, O then they fell a kissing.

John Farmer was an English composer and organist of Holy Trinity (now Christ Church) Cathedral, Dublin, between c.1595 and c.1599, but otherwise lived in London. His madrigals of 1599 are unassuming but attractive, and he supplied many competent 4-part psalm settings for Michael East's (c.1580-1648) and Thomas Ravenscroft's (1583-1633) psalters, and instrumental music for anthologies by Phillip Rosseter (c.1567-1623). He contributed a madrigal "Fair nymphs I heard one teilling *(sic)* " to *The Triumphs of Oriana.*

Overview of the Poem

Faire Phyllis is a six-line poem, less developed and intricate than the sonnets examined earlier in this volume but no less musical or finely wrought, despite its length. The first quatrain is structured by the rhyme scheme (abab); though "alone" and "gone" no longer rhyme in modern English, in Elizabethan English they do rhyme with a long, open "O," like the sound in present day English "caught." The meter of the quatrain is iambic pentameter and is fairly (no pun) regular. The only variations may fall in the first foot: "Faire Phyl-" is a stout spondee, beginning the poem with conviction and emphasis on the name of the beloved. "I saw" may be iambic, but if "I" is also emphasized, then it too is a spondee, obtaining two spondaic feet before the flowing rhythm of the next three iambs. The alliteration on "f" in the first foot is picked up at the start of line two, "feeding," drawing attention to the first sound in the star's name. The first three lines are calmly end-stopped in the quatrain, but line four, despite being sometimes punctuated by modern editors with a period, is enjambed and flows powerfully into the rhyming couplet that ends the poem.

The phrase "up and down" implies wandering and searching, as Amyntas, the male protagonist, searches for his lover. To emphasize the length of his search, the poet has added an extra foot to this line, making it a hexameter, with six feet:

(5) Up and down he wandered whilst she was missing:

"Up and down he wandered" changes the iambic music of the poem with two consecutive trochees, expressing the searching, taking us "up and down" whatever hills and valleys the lover is scouring in search of his "missing" lover. "Missing" not only indicates that she is out of his sight but also that he is "missing" her. Of course "missing" also invites us transparently but no less dramatically to hope for some "kissing" as a final resolution and remedy. We are not disappointed:

(6) When he found her, O then they fell a kissing.

This last line, also in hexameter, is mainly trochaic, and the initial stress has the effect of picking up our ears and our spirits, echoing Amyntas's footsteps as he approaches his lover, once lost and now found. The meter lets stress fall on both syllables of "O then" a dramatic turning point in the center of the line, and an exclamation of anticipation and joy that literally tumbles (falls) into the "kissing" that ends the poem. At this point, the reader is banished and the lovers are left alone. The musical setting will linger over this intimate moment longer than the words can, revealing music's unique contribution to this marriage of text and song.

Voicing

It is not clear from historical sources exactly how many persons sang each voice part. It is known that only one copy of each part-book exists generally for each voice part in a collection set. It would follow that at most a few voices could read off a single part book. The essence of madrigal composition, with its intricate polyphonic writing, and fastidious treatment of text, is that it is an intimate style and requires no instrumental support; instruments tend to cloud the clarity of sound. The exception to this is the fact that madrigals were also sung as vocal solos, with the other vocal parts realized on an accompaniment instrument, such as lute. However, in general, the style is realized unaccompanied by at most a few voices on each vocal part.

Faire Phyllis is set for four voices. One outstanding characteristic of the madrigal is the various permutations of vocal pairings employed by composers. These pairings are the possible permutations available to the composer (SA, ST, SB, SAT, SAB and the like). These include: all 4 voices in imitation or homo-rhythm; 1+3 voices in various combinations; 2+2 in various voice pairings; or a diminution of voices, where only 1, 2, or 3 voice texture is used. Variation in pairings provide for expressive declaration as well as the aural relief provided by the different textures.

We see that *Fair Phyllis* begins with a solo line, followed by a homo-rhythmic response, where all voices are singing the same rhythm simultaneously. The next section is four-voice imitation, with two-voice pairings beginning in m. 12. "Wandering" commences with a three-part scrambling of voices commensurate with a search, but over a "ground-bass" pedal tone. The imagery of this vintage madrigalism is in the unstable painting of the words "up and down" over the stability of the "ground," the terrain.

Other representative pairings of voices commence on the text "whilst she was missing," and simplifies to homo-rhythmic texture on the subsequent "when he found her." And finally, with the metric change of section from duple to triple, the kissing begins with three voices soon becoming the passion of four voices! Such provocative madrigalism is clearly what made this Tudor musical form an engaging entertainment activity.

Tempo

A principle feature of *tactus* structure is that text is set musically in a very speech-like way; and tempo is inherent in speech. The pace at which one recites text is linked directly to expression. Therefore, the tempo of the *tactus* is in fact the tempo of the drama. One finds that within a single large section of a composition composers may vary rhythmic notation, but not *tactus,* to guide changes of expression. On the other hand, the *tactus* might change at a new large section in order to capture the point of new drama.

In *Fair Phyllis* we are given a complete *tactus* on the first whole note, on the word "fair. "[19] (See measure 1) In the following measure further rhythmic division occurs and we begin to set our "groove." It is noted that in numerous compositions from this musical period, both sacred and secular imitative works, the first note of the piece is a single note that fills a measure. It is very possible that this gesture exists only in order to set the *tactus.* But at what pace should the *tactus* be? One manner to determine the tempo of this first note is by looking at a small phrase of text, for example, "sitting all alone." (See measure 3) By repeating these words out loud several times the conductor can play with the syntax of the phrase and decide on a tempo. Setting the pace of the text phrase in this way provides a good prompt for the overall tempo.

Then by virtue of note values, the shepherds seem somewhat confused in the next section of text, "they knew not whither she was gone." (See measure 9) There is no need to change the tempo of the *tactus,* however, throughout this madrigal; the craft of rhythmic notation within each section, with also the same speed of *tactus*, determines the desired contrasts of expression.

This is true for each successive formal section; the context of drama is inherent in the rhythmic notation. One beautiful example is demonstrated in the change from duple to triple meter on the text, "O, then they fell a kissing." No change of *tactus* is needed, only a change of feel within the *tactus,* and this is provided explicitly in the notation (See measure 32), where each direction of the *tactus* in common meter now becomes a complete measure in compound meter. Farmer has captured, in triple time, the sense of two young lovers rolling and playing with their kissing, in contrast to their previous wandering in duple time. This alternation between two musical feels is the "essential to the essence" of a madrigal.

---

[19] By observation of numerous motets and madrigals this author has coined the term "'O' gesture" for the length of the first note frequently beginning these works. Typically the first note is a whole note in the first measure, followed by smaller divisions of the whole note in following measures: whole note, two half-notes, quarter notes with eighth notes, and the like. The term is named for the fact that the whole note is often on the word "O," as in the texts "<u>O</u> magnum mysterium...," "<u>O</u> vos omnes...," or "<u>O</u> quam gloriosum...."

Phrasing and Stress

Phrasing in great music is logical, and rhetorical. Phrasing is also one of the most explicit decisions that composers communicate in their notation. It is not the intention of composers to trick performers, in the hope of being profound. If this were the case regular misinterpretation would be designed into their performances.

> ...it is essential to give attention to the relative strength of points of arrival in order to make effective decisions regarding phrasing and pacing.

Rather, phrasing in the madrigal is logical and falls generally into the scheme of the *tactus.* To sing each voice part, in the context of the *tactus,* will unfold phrasing, as well as to provide the aural information necessary to assign points of harmonic arrival. It is important to place the singing of madrigals into their historic context; singers read part books. Even though today's singers have the advantage of a score, the essence is that each part is distinguished from the others. Establish a tempo, and then using the physical gesture of the *tactus* sing each part.

Pay special attention to the syncopation, and recognize such notation as an important expressive opportunity. The treatises are clear that syncopation is a frequent devise. It is not recommended that conductors find places to impose expression, however it is essential that moments of expression be recognized, and not ignored. Again, syncopation allows for rhetorical shifts to occur in an otherwise mundane metric pattern; it is an element from speech, which distinguishes a fine orator from a common speaker. Most importantly, syncopation is not a coincidence, but rather an intention from the composer.

Examples of syncopation occur: (1) on the homo-rhythmic word "flock" in measure 5; (2) "lover" in the soprano and alto parts in measures 13-14; (3) "up" in the alto part in measures 23-24; and (4) "when" in the alto part measures 30-31.

Points of arrival[20] assist the conductor in both the analysis of the formal structure and the pacing of performance. These points are heard within the context of harmony and exist in relative strengths. For example, there is a stronger point of arrival to the tonic tone, approached from the dominant tone above, than to the tonic from the lower dominant degree. There is a weaker point of arrival to the mediant or dominant tones of a given tonality, and certainly to the arrival of other diatonic tones. Again, strength of arrival is relative and calls upon the judgment of the conductor.

It is recommended that while singing each vocal part the conductor place a mark, such as **V**, over each point of arrival in the line.[21] After all vocal lines have been assigned their points of arrival some important conclusions can be made. The more

---

[20] "Point of arrival" is in contrast to "cadence," where two or more voices arrive at the same vertical time. Point of arrival refers to any single line within a voice part that comes to rest.

[21] For an excellent discussion on the procedures of analysis in the music of the Renaissance see Dennis Shrock's article in *Choral Essays: A Tribute to Roger Wagner.*

points of arrival that occur at any vertical point, then the stronger the cadence, the more stable the moment. The fewer points of arrival at any vertical moment, the less stable the moment. It follows that stronger cadence points require more dissipation of energy, more "stop" to the musical direction, while a point of arrival in only a single voice would not interrupt the musical direction at all. Such analysis assists the conductor in bringing a sense of pacing to the performance, guided by the music.

In *Fair Phyllis* the strong cadences fall on: (1) measure 7 and again on the repeat at measure 8; (2) measure 32; (3) its repeat; and (4) the final cadence. Each of these strong cadences fall on the principle formal points, and require that special attention be given at these moments. It also follows that less important arrival points exist for all other points of arrival. Measure 18 could be seen as a strong cadence, however the tenor voice arrives on the dominant tone and the syncopation of movement to "up and down" turns this more into a three-voice cadence, with less musical "stop." Throughout the "wandered" section, measures 18-28, there are only single-voice points of arrival, while the section ends at measure 28 with a cadence of paired voices. To review, it is essential to give attention to the relative strength of the points of arrival in order to make effective decisions regarding phrasing and pacing.

Articulation

Articulation is the word given to the quality of a single note, and can refer to resultant stress, tone, dynamic shading (*messa da voce),* and length, as in *staccato* or *tenuto*.

For the sake of vocabulary, *legato* is not articulation, but rather a quality of phrasing, since the connection is between two or more notes. The common articulation of the Renaissance, and continuing into the Baroque period, is that of "more detached than connected." We might use as our model for sound ideal the lute, which was a popular accompanying instrument. The flow of words within a madrigal tends to be the continuum of individual articulations, matched to the length of a plucked tone. At the same time, the overall sweet sound avoids an overly harsh onset of vocal tone.

The common articulation of the Renaissance, and continuing into the Baroque period, is that of "more detached than connected."

This general length of articulation does not limit vocal possibilities, but rather opens the door for extreme subtleness. Each note contributes to either build or to dissipate a musical phrase; in fact the idea here is to make the singing of a madrigal equal to the finest rhetorical quality of speech, but to further enhance the musical quality of words with music itself.

Fair Phyllis is rich with opportunity to explore the breadth of expressive articulation and its contribution to the building of phrase. Please accept that all expression comes from the musical source, from the poetry and the composition. For example, the first word "Fair" and its spondee partner, "Phyl-lis" are notated to denote explicitly the desired articulation: "Fair" is a whole note and will be sung on a complete *tactus,* with *messa da voce.* The importance given to this first sonic representation of the text cannot be overstated. "Phyl-lis," is notated much shorter and sets up directly in the speech rhythm of the tempo. The articulation of the second note will be detached, shorter than the lengthy and deliberately shaped first note. No better example can be found to illuminate the intention of contrasting articulation between adjacent notes.

Predominately, the motion of the text here warrants a speech-like, detached, articulation. However, the text also requires that certain words carry the accentuation of syntax, that one syllable be longer than another. For example, the alternation, beginning in m. 18 on the text, "up and down he wandered," of stress on "up" or "down" creates an added layer of searching, of instability, that is concomitant with the textual meaning.

And, multiple syntax can occur even simultaneously. For example in m. 13, "But after her lover," the alto anacrusis sets up "af-ter" as the syllable (word) of syntactical stress; the soprano, in contrast, with the word "But" on the crucis of the *tactus,* places the stress on a different word. Referring to an earlier footnote, this juxtaposition of stress can confuse even the logic of textual meaning. What must be determined first is the intended meaning, "But after her, lover Amyntas heid." (As an aside, this is also the resultant stress of the FIRST statement of the imitated phrase.) Then, the subsequent lines can be experienced in opposition to the first; pithy.

Finally, the phrase that begins in m. 31, "O, then they fell a-kissing," again accents the importance of articulation (built upon word stress) to the marriage of text and music. "O" and "then" are both stressed poetic syllables and longer shaped musical lengths, in contrast to shorter note values on other words. However, these lovers are not simply rocking dolls, moving regularly forward and back. Their pace of kissing varies within shifting note values and syncopated rhythm. This passion is not superficial; it is intense.

Tone Quality

A natural vocal sound is ideal for the singing of madrigals. However, this does not imply "white" sound, without vibrato. All good singing results in the gentle undulation of the voice that is vibrato. The texts call upon the singer to draw from one's human passions, with warmth and affection, love and despair. Treatises repeat the call for "sweetness" in vocal sound, and the use of "good taste" in both stylistic decisions and vocal production.

Dynamics

Simply stated, dynamic markings are not written generally in manuscript sources of the madrigals. It is assumed, however, that shades of volume would be expected. Treatises speak of dynamics as a principle tool for the interpretation of text. Since most texts are narrative, it is common that the dynamics would be moderate, and not explore the extremes to excess. The guidance would again be "good taste."

The story of Phyllis is told in first person by an impartial, perhaps unseen, observer, calling generally for a subdued speech-like dynamic. Also, the confused state of mind of Amyntas not knowing where Phyllis is, as well as his searching "up and down" for her do not conjure strong dynamics. In fact, the dynamic context of the entire poem falls on the gentle side, some text even more gentle than other. The soft nature of this madrigal can be seen perhaps in the context of our observer not wanting to be overheard while telling another person (or us) about Phyllis and Amyntas.

Selected Example #2: Suggestions for Preparation and Performance
***The Silver Swan* (Orlando Gibbons 1583-1625) ed. William Belan with special contributions by Michael Calabrese**
***Gentry Publications,* Catalogue No. JG2368**

The silver swan,
who living had no note,
When death approached unlocked her silent throat;
Leaning her breast against the reedy shore,
Thus sung her first and last, and sung no more:
Farewell, all joys;
O death, come close mine eyes;
More geese than swans now live,
more fools than wise.

THE SILVER SWAN

ORLANDO GIBBONS (1583-1625)
Edited by
WILLIAM BELAN

*The keyboard part is not a reduction of the vocal lines, but rather an idiomatic realization for aid in the learning process.

4
5
6
S
note, When death ap-proached un - locked her si - lent
A
When death ap-proached un - locked her si - lent
A2
note, When death ap-proached un - locked her si - lent
T
note, When death ap - proached un - locked her si - lent
B
note, When death ap - proached un - locked her si - lent, si - lent
7
8
9
S
throat; Lean - ing her breast a -
A
throat; Lean - ing her breast a - gainst the reed - y
A2
throat; Lean - ing her breast a - gainst the
T
throat; A - gainst the reed - y shore,
B
throat; Lean - ing her breast a - gainst the reed - y

10
11
12
S
gainst the reed - y shore, Thus sung her first and
A
shore, Thus sung her first and last, and sung no
A2
reed - y shore, Thus sung her first and last and
T
Thus sung her first and last, and sung no more, and sung
B
shore, Thus sung her first and last, and
13
14
15
last, and sung no more: Fare - well, all
more, no more: Fare - well all joys, O
sung no more: Fare - well all joys, O
no more: Fare - well all joys, O
sung no more: Fare - well all joys, O

16
17
18
S
joys, O death, come close mine eyes; More
A
death, come close mine eyes; More geese than swans now
A2
death, come close mine eyes; More geese than swans
T
death, come close mine eyes; More geese than
B
death come close mine eyes; More geese than
19
20
21
S
geese than swans now live, more fools than wise.
A
live, more fools than wise, than wise.
A2
now live, more fools than wise.
T
swans now live, more fools than wise.
B
swans now live, more fools than wise.

The silver swan,
who living had no note,
When death approached unlocked her silent throat;
Leaning her breast against the reedy shore,
Thus sung her first and last, and sung no more:
Farewell, all joys;
O death, come close mine eyes;
More geese than swans now live,
more fools than wise.

Orlando Gibbons belongs to the generation of English composers that followed that of William Byrd, forty years his senior, who had died in 1623. He was a chorister at King's College, Cambridge, where his elder brother was Master of the Choristers, and later became a gentleman of the Chapel Royal, which he served as an organist and to which he later added the position of organist at Westminster Abbey. He wrote music for the Church of England, madrigals, consort music and keyboard works. [22]

Overview of the Poem

The *Silver Swan* is a six-line poem, made up of three rhyming couplets (aabbcc). The meter is generally iambic pentameter, with some dramatic variation. "Leaning" is a trochee (– **u**), if not a spondee (– –), emphasizing the physical action of the musical bird, forcing us to linger on the liquid "l" and nasal" "–n" and "–ng." Here is a vivid example of bringing an aesthetic into the poem, treating the word "leaning" with the imagination of sound, experimenting with accentuation, and literally feeling the results of each test. Further, each line of the poem is end stopped, as each action proceeds deliberately and patiently.

But what is the poem about? It recounts the dying moments in the life of a swan, a real animal but one with a host of mythic associations to poetry, inspiration and song. The mythos of a "swan song" is well known; the swan is a silent bird that sings only before death. The first two couplets exploit this tragic drama, depicting the bird's first and final performance. "S" sounds dominate these couplets, as do the sounds of long "e" and long "o," both open ("shore" and "more") and closed ("note" and "throat"). Sonically, the poet is allowing us to hear the sound of song as it emerges from the long-silent throat of the dying bird. The thumping regular iambs of line four depict the death of the swan, compelling us to fall with her, just as we had "leaned" upward and "unlocked" our throats with her a moment ago. The "u" and "o" sounds of the last three words create a hauntingly howling lamentation: "sung no more." The final couplet completely leaves the swan behind and takes us into the bitter world of the poet, who wants to die, like the swan.

In complex ways, the poet sees himself in the swan: perhaps he has been un-recognized and un-appreciated by a fickle public and thus has been, metaphorically,

---

[22] http://www.hnh.com/composers/gibbons.htm

"silent" in his career? Perhaps the geese, cackling, opportunistic (but no doubt lesser) poets have drowned him out, leading him now to wish for death so that he will finally be heard? The couplet is ambiguous, but its tone is not: the poet is full of rancor. The imagery and shift in tone make the deceptively simple verses difficult and exciting to hear, as we wonder what a "swan song" will sound like and how can music express the poet's own sorrows and frustrations, struggling as a silver swan in a world of geese.

Voicing

The opening seven measures of *The Silver Swan* bring the five-voice writing (two treble voices and three men's voices) into consort, beginning and ending in homo-rhythmic texture, while working together to set the premise for the poem, that the silver swan makes no sound during its life, but when approaching death the swan's tone is finally preparing to sing. The remainder of this short madrigal is more imitative, however never really explores vocal pairings to any extreme degree. There are subtle moments when pairs of voices exist, for example in measure 7 in the alto and bass; in measure 14 in the alto and bass; and in measure 16 in the alto and tenor. However, throughout the madrigal the texture remains very stable, the voices never establish any pattern of pairings that distracts from its simple story, or its internal meaning.

Tempo

The tempo here never needs to vary from the first *tactus* to the last, and the tempo is determined easily by the first dotted rhythmic in measures 2-3, "who living had no note. To recite out loud this phrase of text in rhythm several times provides everything one needs to know about the tempo. We can then distribute this *tactus* across the entire work. Every subsequent change of expression is managed beautifully by the composer with his choice of note values, and placement of syncopation. Tempo does not need to change; rather, one only explores the adjustment of rhythm and text placement within the *tactus;* this little jewel then shines.

Phrasing and Stress

The composition begins with a poignant madrigalism built into the phrasing, for in the first seven measures, the swan, "who living had no note," also has no harmonic points of arrival in any of its five voices, emphasizing that there is here also no important "note." Such a creative moment is a beautiful example of the depth in which madrigalism functions.

However, in measure 7 all voices cadence directly, preparing for another madrigalism. The next word, "leaning," is realized immediately upon a strong syncopation, first in the alto/bass vocal pairing, and again in syncopation by a tenor and soprano pairing, creating a musical effect that is itself "leaning."

To highlight another madrigalism in phrasing, this same syncopation figure in measure 7 is repeated in measure 14, on the words "farewell, all joys." We might conclude that the composer's interpretation of the swan's "leaning" is equated to its feeling of "farewell" to joy. Madrigalism has again provided a window into the interpretive insight of the composer, who used rhythmic syncopation to illuminate textual meaning.

Beginning the final couplet of the poem in measure 17, "More geese than swans..." is colored also by phrasing. For the *stretto*[23] placement of the word "geese" against the *tactus* gives the impression of squawking, especially as the word "geese" itself has a very bright vowel formant, in comparison to the word "swans" which follows in each entrance two notes later. "Swans" carries a vowel sound that is much richer and darker. The parallelism of the final line of the poem is now clear; the squawking of the "fools" in contrast to the sonic richness of the "wise." The phrase, and its essential *tactus,* again provides the canvas upon which the composer imprints his view of the poem. Phrasing is used as a strong expressive tool, providing for a depth of meaning not easily represented by more surface features. The conductor must now probe these depths to realize the madrigal's full potential.

Tone Quality

An important thesis presented throughout this handbook is that poetry and music are a marriage, that although clearly differentiated they are, to quote a Buddhist analogy, "as close as two sides of the same sheet of paper." One thing, however, is clear; the poem precedes the musical setting. The composer uses the poem as a muse, calling upon the poem's craft to inspire the composition. As conductors we re-create (or to play upon words, recreate) this marriage. And it must be reiterated that little of value here is by coincidence.

The reading aloud of our poem highlights an important opportunity for the performance of the madrigal. Only a handful of words cipher by their quality of sound: death; leaning; reedy; farewell; death (again); geese; and fools. By the nature of an aggressive consonant or brighter vowel these particular words penetrate an otherwise mellow reading. Here then the conductor has a roadmap for expression; to affect the musical tone quality on these select words lifts the interpretation of the poem.

Dynamics

The definition of "dynamic"[24] in music is assumed generally to be primarily that of loud to soft. However, dynamics is more than volume only. In the Renaissance we see

---

[23] In *stretto* writing, the successive statements of a theme are presented very close together in time.

[24] Only one of six definitions in the Macintosh *English Dictionary* (version 10.0) mentions "volume." A broader view is that of "energy," "enthusiasm," "sense of purpose," characterized by "vigorous activity," and "any system that changes over time."

dynamics from the large dimension to the smallest dimension, from the quality of a formal section to the quality of a single note. Examples of small scale dynamic are the articulation of *messa da voce,* the lengthening of a note with accentuation (without over-emphasizing amplitude), or the resultant contrast between one vowel/consonant and another. And this is especially important to note when looking at a madrigal because the poems also function at these various levels.

The general volume of *The Silver Swan* is at most moderate, and no specific section of the madrigal is "loud," although there is perhaps a call for contrast in volume. The repeat of the syncopated section, m. 14, on the word "farewell" can be softer, continuing through the death of the swan. The last line of the poem might return then to the moderate narrative volume. Although not excessive, such shaping of amplitude is welcome.

All of the small-scale dynamic shadings are present also in this setting. *Messa da voce* exists on notes of length; "swan" in m. 2, "ap-proached" in the tenor of m. 5, for example, as well as the syncopated words "lean-ing" and "fare-well."

Notes of more regular length that fall on the "crusis" of the *tactus* provide contrast, perceived as dynamic. The first measure begins with an anacrusis followed by a stress of *tactus* on "sil-ver" and again on "swan" in the second measure. These points of accentuation are not principally by volume, but by syllabic length, *agogic* accents; they carry the stress of the word.

And finally, the words of special color that cipher in the reading of the text also carry dynamic quality. They possess inherent energy, and most of all hold special purpose in the meaning of the poem, which qualify them in the category of "dynamics." The conductor continues to pursue essential details, to teach these rhetorical effects to the singers, and to bring the potential of the madrigal to eager listeners.

Conclusion

The marriage of music and text in the English madrigal was not so much historical coincidence, but rather opportunity. And the fact that poets recognized the status of musicians while musicians recognized the same status of poets at the same time brought about a remarkable exploitation of this good fortune. For a brief half century musicians set the texts of wordsmiths that has resulted in one of vocal music's most treasured *opera.*

The task of the madrigal conductor is to understand from each selection the essential stylistic information of both music and poetry, to internalize the inherent "music of the word" and the "words in the music." To reiterate, insightful interpretation is not a factor of intuition alone, but also the labor of vision and knowledge. From the primary-source writings of contemporary madrigal musicians we have inherited insights about the music, explanations about the essential components of *tactus* and expression. From the writings of madrigal poets we have their collected works and accompanying briefings. As the modern conductor seeks to unbundled and apply this information one is afforded a sort of interpretive vision, a glimpse into the pursuit of truth. We may not ever be able to declare that truth has been fulfilled, but at least we have earned the right to perform a "latest misinterpretation."

GLOSSARY OF TERMS

Agogic accent - the syllable that carries the stress of a word

Breve - equal to the modern music note that is two whole note in length

Cadence - a short sequence of notes that mark the end of a phrase, also called "close," which must occur in two lines of music simultaneously (see *point of arrival)*

Chironomy - the system of hand signs used in conducting, from the words "chiros" (Greek) meaning "hands," and the suffix "nomy," meaning a system

Coda - an additional section at the end of a text that brings added dramatic energy to the close

Counterpoint - musical composition that sets one musical voice in opposition to another

Couplet - two lines of verse that form a unit alone or as part of a poem, especially two that rhyme and have the same meter

Enjambment - the continuation of meaning, without pause of break, from one line of poetry to the next

Iamb - a unit of rhythm in poetry (foot), consisting of one short or unstressed syllable followed by one long or stressed syllable, for example, the word "hu<u>mane</u>"

Incipit - the opening word or words of a text

Kinesthetic quality - the perception or sensing of the motion, weight, or position of the hands in conducting, or of a musical idea within the measure.

Mensuration - the calculation of musical note quantity, such as with various lengths of musical notes and their relationship to one another

Messa da voce (Italian) - an articulation in which the singer becomes louder and softer on a single note

Poetic foot - a basic unit or rhythm in poetry, made up of a fixed combination of stressed and unstressed or long and short syllables

Poetic meter - an arranged pattern of rhythm in a line of poetry

Poetic octave - a verse of poetry consisting of eight lines

Poetic sestet - a verse of poetry consisting of six lines

Point of arrival - similar to a cadence but occurring in only a single line of music (see *cadence)*

Quatrain - a verse of poetry consisting of four lines, frequently one with lines that rhyme alternately

Semi-breve - equal to the modern whole note in length

Sonnet form - a short poem with fourteen lines, usually ten-syllable rhyming lines, divided into two-three, or four sections

Spondee - a unit of rhythm in poetry (foot), consisting of two long or stressed syllables, used as an exaggeration

Stretto - in an imitative style of music, the successive statements of the theme very close together in time

Syncopation - a rhythmic technique in music in which the accept is shifted to a weak beat of the bar

Tactus - the rhythmic organization of music in a "down-up" or "down-down-up" pattern

Trochee - a unit of rhythm in poetry (foot) that consists of one stressed syllable followed by an unstressed syllable, for example, the word "<u>hu</u>man"

Verse format - poetry as opposed to prose; a particular form of poetry

BIBLIOGRAPHY

Belan, William, ed. *Choral Essays: A Tribute to Roger Wagner.* San Carlos, CA: Thomas House Publications, 1993. S.v. "Gregorian Musical Words" by M. Clement Morin, and "Music in the Renaissance" by Dennis Shrock.

Douglas Bush and Alfred Harbage, ed.. *Shakespeare's Sonnets.* Baltimore: Penguin, 1961.

Cardine, Dom Eugene. *Gregorian Semiology,* trans. Robert M. Fowells. Solesmes, France: Abbye St.-Pierre de Solesmes, 1982.

Couper-Kuhlen, Elizabeth. *An Introduction to English Prosody.* Tübingen: M. Niemeyer, 1986.

The Critical Tradition: Classic Texts and Contemporary Trends, ed. David H. Richter. Boston and New York: Bedford/St. Martins, 1998.

Fellowes, Edmund H. *The English Madrigal Composers,* 2nd ed. London: Oxford and New York, University Press, 1948.

_____. *The English Madrigal.* London and New York: Oxford University Press, 1925.

Fish, Stanley. *Professional Correctness: Literary Study and Political Change.* Oxford: Clarendon, 1995.

Jacobs, Charles. *Tempo Notation in Renaissance Spain.* Brooklyn: Institute of Medieval Music, 1964.

Ledger, Philip, ed. *The Oxford Book of English Madrigals.* Oxford and New York: Oxford University Press, 1978.

Norton Introduction to Poetry, Shorter Fourth Edition, ed. Margaret Ferguson et al. New York: Norton, 1102-22.

Pound, Ezra. *ABC of Reading.* New York: New Directions, 1960.

Raffel, Burton, *From Stress to Stress: an Autobiography of English Prosody.* Hamden, Conn.: Archon books, 1992.

Sylvester, Richard S. ed. *English Sixteenth-Century Verse.* New York and London: Norton, 1974.

.250 Poems: A Portable Anthology, ed. Peter Schakel and Jack Ridl. Boston and New York: Bedford/St. Martins, 2003.

About the Authors

Dr. William Belan

Dr. William Belan is Professor of Music and Director of Choral Studies at California State University, Los Angeles where he also directs the Roger Wagner Center for Choral Studies. Dr. Belan is a reader at both the Huntington Library (San Marino, California) and the Library of Congress (Washington D.C.). His first book, *Choral Essays: A Tribute to Roger Wagner*, was published in 1995 (Thomas House Publications).

Dr. Michael Calabrese

Michael Calabrese is Professor of English in the English Department at California State University, Los Angeles. He is the author of Chaucer's *Ovidian Arts of Love*, published by the University Press of Florida, and he has written numerous articles on medieval English and Continental literature, including work on Chaucer, Langland, the Gawain Poet, Boccaccio, and on Marie de France. He is one of the editors of the Piers Plowman Electronic Archive , creating electronic scholarly editions of *Piers Plowman* manuscripts housed at the Huntington Library (San Marino, California).